PSYCHOLOGICAL FOUNDATIONS OF THE ARTS: UNDERSTANDING AND ENCOURAGING ARTISTIC EXPRESSION IN THE EARLY GRADES

Erin Morris Miller
and
Rachael Sloan

Cheryll M. Adams, Series Editor

National Association for Gifted Children

1331 H Street, NW, Suite 1001

Washington, DC 20005

202-785-4268

http://www.nagc.org

TABLE OF CONTENTS

INTRODUCTION

Many educators are surprised to discover that there is an entire branch of psychology devoted to the study of the arts that is in addition to and separate from the study of creativity. Like most areas of psychology, the study of the arts involves a wide range of topics including cognitive and biological studies, clinical investigations, and exploration of personality. Psychologists not only study the artists themselves, they also study the experience of the audience, which is the area of aesthetics. Substantial artistic contributions are rare, but anyone can be a part of an audience and the experience of art. Rudolf Arnheim, one of the most influential psychologists in the area of artistic perception, saw all psychological processes as having cognitive, motivational, and emotional aspects as well as cultural interaction and a dialogue between the artist and the audience.[1] Thus, in this branch of psychology the focus can be on the study of the artist, the study of the person experiencing the art, or both.

These two orientations to the study of art in psychology provide fertile ground for teachers wishing to achieve the dual goals of exploring the arts in the classroom with all children and supporting the development of those children and adolescents who demonstrate talent in the arts. A teacher may have only a few students who will go on to become professional artists, musicians, actors, or writers/composers, but everyone can experience art, listen to music, and watch movies or plays. Most people do at least one of these regularly during their lives. Thus, the focus of this book is not on prodigies who are already performing at the expert level, rather those students who may have the potential for expert performance in adulthood. This text explores the range of perspectives regarding the relatively new area called the psychological foundation of the arts.

The focus of this text is on three domains of the arts: music, tactile art, and the theater. In the discussion of the artists themselves we describe the cognitive and brain structure differences, development, personality, and clinical issues that are important to understanding budding artists. The discussion of aesthetics explores the relationship between the art and the person experiencing art and focuses on encouraging teachers to facilitate a love of the arts in all their students. Following the discussion of what we know about artists and the aesthetic experience, we provide implications for the classroom.

COGNITIVE AND BIOLOGICAL ASPECTS

Just what makes the artist/musician/actor differ from others? How do these remarkable individuals do what they do? Studies from the perspective of cognitive and biological psychology can give us insight into how the brains of artistic individuals are different from non-artists. For example, why can some people draw realistically and others cannot? In order to draw realistically one must perceive the vase as it exists in space, decide which areas of the vase to draw and how to represent those areas, have the fine motor coordination to render those decisions graphically, objectively analyze the accuracy of these marks, and correct errors. Individuals can differ in each of these steps.

Tactile Arts

In order to create art the first step is to perceive what one wants to represent. Perception is the study of how the human brain interprets information coming from the five senses (sight, hearing, touch, smell, taste.). The information coming into one's eyes, ears, and nose is the same for everyone. But the way each person's brain interprets that information is unique. Perhaps talented visual artists are able to create realistic drawings because they literally perceive the world differently than non-artists. There are two possible explanations for this: the bottom-up and the top-down approaches.[2] Bottom-up cognitive control is when people build up their understanding from the individual elements of what they perceive. According to the bottom-up approach artists achieve clearer perception by ignoring the information from their brains about what things should look like and perceiving the shapes, shadows, and lines as they are. Artists can draw what they see; not what they know. Another way to explain it is that artists see what their eyes are taking in -- not what their brains expect.

The top-down approach is knowledge driven. It depends on previous knowledge and expectations based on experience. The ability of some individuals to accurately depict what they see is the result of artists' ability to use their knowledge and understanding of line, shape and shadow. Artists use specialized knowledge about drawing (or painting or sculpture, etc.) that helps them isolate the important features. The key question is, "When we look into the world, do we focus what we take in through our senses or do we "see" only what we know?" Shifting how we understand the world from the conceptual level to the perceptual is not easy.

Acting

However, shifting from the perceptual to the conceptual is not easy either. In contrast to the tactile arts, success in the physical arts, such as acting, is not a matter of accurate perception of surface features, but an ability to ignore surface features and see the inner cognitive processes. When analyzing text, the goal of actors is to extract the inner motivations of the assigned characters from the literal words of the text. Top down cognitive processes seem to be more important to actors than to visual artists[3]. For example, professional actors tend to use every learning principle that has been identified by cognitive researchers as facilitating recall: elaboration, depth of processing, distinctiveness, causal attribution, perspective taking, and overlearning. Of course acting is more cognitively sophisticated than simple recall of lines. In addition to memory one needs sensitivity to emotions, ability to imagine others' mental states (theory of mind) and awareness of the intricacies of the character's underlying psychology, a powerful imagination, strong verbal memory, and the ability to imitate. Actors must use all their physical, mental, and emotional channels to ensure that the audience perceives what the actor intends.

Acting is a cognitively complex process that does not necessarily come naturally, but seems to have its roots in childhood preferences. However, very little is known about those cognitive and biological roots.

There is some evidence to suggest that during childhood, actors show early verbal memory ability and an attraction to fiction's world of imagination and emotionality. Gifted actors recall being able to mimic, memorize verbal texts, and engage in creating theatre at an early age.[4] The "class clown" may be a stereotype of future actors, but most actors recall simply being bored in school.

Music

In contrast, musical ability is intriguing because it is both quite natural to human beings and cognitively complex. Unlike other arts, there is more shared commonality of performance; almost everyone sings at least a little and many people who are not professional musicians sing and listen to music every day. Even without much practice, the ordinary adult has the basic cognitive and biological abilities that are necessary to sing simple songs. All humans have musical knowledge as a result of day-to-day experiences with the music of their culture.[5] For the average person there are no perceptual or conceptual barriers to the production of music. Even if one is unable to speak due to a neurological disability, one can still use one's voice to produce the notes of music. However there are certainly physical characteristics that can facilitate or inhibit the ability to play an instrument or use one's voice such as: pitch discrimination/control, physical size, and hand size/shape. All these factors play a role in determining whether one can develop expertise in the production of music. There are individual differences in abilities to perceive pitch, timbre, tempo, and rhythm as well as individual differences in musical memory and tracking of harmonic structure. It is these initial abilities that might first distinguish the talented child or adolescent from others. Musical ability is both a natural part of our biological design and an area in which individuals differ in perceptual ability.

Implications for the Classroom

Despite the physical or perceptual abilities involved, teachers can help students to develop the cognitive skills needed to be better artists, actors, and musicians. First and foremost, remember that the mind is constantly developing. Abilities are not static. Students should be taught the specific skills of artistic production, performance, and music. Teachers often make the mistake of singling out the student who seems to have a "natural gift" for the arts and then providing additional practice and experiences for only those students. This is unfortunate as the human mind is so receptive to the change and development that results from deliberate practice. At the same time it is essential that the teacher also recognize that even those students who seem to have a natural talent need instruction and practice. The following sample applications can be used with both students who have the motivation, abilities, and interest that characterize a talented child and those students who may still be developing their abilities and interests.

In order to develop the cognitive skills involved in the visual arts, teachers should consider integrating perceptual exercises into their curriculum. For example, during a lesson on the types of clouds, one could integrate an activity where the students were asked to identify the type of clouds in the sky and then write down all the shapes that they see. This would lead to a discussion of how all people see things differently and are unique. Then the children would create drawings that included each type of cloud to be studied but using the shapes that they perceived in the sky. Another possibility is to use extreme close-up photographs or images. One use of this technique is in the study of ancient civilizations and in particular ancient Greece. Part of an extreme close-up of the capital of a column is provided and the student is to complete the picture. This provides experience not only with identifying the different styles of capitals, but also with looking at shapes through a different perspective.

Changing perceptions is important to acting, but in quite a different way. Actors must be able to embody the perspective of another person. The exploration of compelling literature is one of the key ways that teachers can allow students to practice taking on different perspectives and provide opportunities to explore different characters. Techniques such as Reader's Theater allow students to practice these skills.[6] Students might even write from the perspective of an object, as in the RAFT writing template, in which students must decide on the role of the writer, the audience of the work, the format of the work, and the topic. This writing might occur in the form of a poem, a diary entry, a movie script, or any of the many other formats of writing.[7] For example, students could write about the Constitutional Convention of 1787 from the perspective of the pen used by James Madison to take notes. Students may be directed to re-write works of literature from the perspective of minor characters. Another possibility is to encourage recitation of a poem with clear emotional content from different points of view (e.g., students recite a poem from the perspective of the person experiencing the emotion and then recite it again with sarcasm).

Sortiropoulou-Zormpala[8] describes an innovative kindergarten classroom in which phonemes and graphemes of letters are taught through different aesthetic experiences that involve directing children to change their perspectives. In one activity the children pretend that they are citizens of countries who speak various languages consisting of one repeated vowel sound. The teacher whispers the assigned sound into the child's ear. With their eyes closed, children slowly mingle repeating their sound until they have found all the members of their country. This metaphor of the "one sound country" is then carried through several lessons and the study of phonemes and graphemes is extended into various artistic domains such as theater, music, drawing, and photography. The students experience how emotions, actions and meanings are changed when there is a change in perspective.

Actors also have strong verbal memory and powerful imaginations. Imagination and verbal memory are traits in which individual students will vary. Exceptional memory and imagination is often seen in children who have been identified as intellectually gifted. But, memory is a skill that can be improved even for the most able child. Students can be directly taught strategies that improve recall; such as elaboration and depth of processing. Elaboration is when a student embellishes the information to be recalled with other relevant information. If the embellishments lead to many different and varied connections across all areas of your brain (verbal, visual, tactile, past memories, current experiences, imagined situations, etc.) then one is accomplishing increased depth of processing. For example, Sprague and Bryan[9] describe a middle school math teacher whose students convert factor trees to hanging mobiles with differing mediums used to represent the factors. They also describe a science teacher who has her students create models of cells using a variety of materials seeking to recreate the texture and shape of the cell and organelles. Cognitive skills such as depth of processing are not only important to the theater but also will increase recall across all areas of study.

Many conclusions about the biological and cognitive characteristics of talented musicians, artists, and actors discussed thus far are drawn from studies of adults. Observing a difference in adults does not completely answer the questions about how individuals with talent in the arts differ from other individuals. This type of research does not indicate whether these differences are due to innate differences or training. Did actors, artists, and musicians start out this way or did their training change them? In order to answer this type of question one must look to another area of psychology: life-span human development.

DEVELOPMENT OF ARTISTIC ABILITY

The most accurate way to measure development is to study a large group of people starting in infancy. You could then see which ones become artists and which do not and look back over all the information you gathered to look for differences in how they developed. Unfortunately, the number of infants needed to complete that kind of study would have to be extremely large because professional artists are such a small percentage of the general population. Professional artists at the top of their field are rare for a reason. Throughout the developmental trajectory many small but necessary factors result in the realization of potential as a whole. It is multiplicative not additive, one missing factor means the end result is failure to achieve the stature of eminent professional. Princeton University estimated that one percent of the U.S. population is a professional in the performing and visual arts.[10] This means to be able to study 30 adults who are professional artists (all visual and performing arts combined) one would have to begin with at least 6,000 infants.

Because of the challenges of doing this kind of research, most of what we know about the development of artistic ability comes from studies of successful artistic individuals who reflect upon their childhoods. One consistent theme in the study of the development of artists is a change in focus over time. Children go through stages in their development in any domain including the arts. Early childhood is a time of playful interaction with all types of artistic media and performance possibilities in order to explore fundamental expressive abilities. Middle childhood into adolescence is often a time of applying these expressive abilities in order to achieve competence. It is a time of hard work and practicing of skills. Some theorists propose that proper training and deliberate practice is more powerful than any genetic factor in ensuring success.[11] In adulthood, one must develop mastery and learn how to make a unique contribution. According to Kogan,[12] a shift must take place in adulthood when after years of focused effort and learning of skills, the individual must embrace the artistic professions, despite the realities that few people are able to create a sustained livelihood in the arts. This makes sense as it is only those individuals who do not allow themselves to get discouraged who will become artists in any domain.

Implications for the Classroom

Teachers by nature are sensitive to developmental issues, but these issues can take a back seat in a world that emphasizes the high stakes of educational success. All primary and early elementary students should have the opportunity to experience all of the arts in an environment that emphasizes exploration and fun. At this point in development, if an experience is not enjoyable students are not going to be interested in further participation. This is not to say that there is no structure to the lesson, but rather that there is less concern about the "right way" to sing or draw or perform and more openness to allowing the children to find personal joy. The time for serious study of the conventions of the field is when children are moving through upper elementary and into middle school. Teachers at this stage need to help the students develop the basic competencies required. It is at this point that the talented child should first be discovering if they have (or are interested in developing) the motivation to be a professional artist. Depending on the field, this time of intense study may continue through high school and college. Adulthood is when future artists make the decision to embrace their field. Although most teachers are not providing a direct influence at that moment; teachers' attitudes and messages about careers in the arts continue to influence students. It is important not to discourage students or attempt to redirect their talents and energies towards what may seem more traditional or fiscally safe goals. Never trying is much more tragic than trying and failing. And the challenges that certainly will be faced can be beneficial, as can be seen in the study of the personalities of successful artists.

ARTISTIC CREATION AND PERSONALITY TRAITS

There is much research on the personality characteristics associated with creativity. Certain occupations are inherently creative such as musicians, artists, novelists, and actors. For the purpose of an explanation of the psychology of the arts, this section is limited to studies with the arts population alone. One issue that must be considered is that people with the same personality profile do not embark on the same career path. The big question regarding this type of work is the following: Is the characteristic a cause or product of a visual or performing arts career? In other words, do certain personalities lead one to become an artist or does being an artist lead one to develop a certain personality?

One way to study personality in artists is to compare artists to non-artists without consideration of creativity. Artists, as a group, when compared to non-artists, are less cautious, conscientious, controlled, orderly, and reliable. Artists tend to be more aesthetic, creative, curious, imaginative, open to experiences, sensitive, and original. Artists are usually less conventional, rigid, and socialized, meaning that they are more likely to challenge convention. Artists are more likely to be aggressive, cold, egocentric, impulsive, and tough-minded.[13] It is possible that individuals with these traits are likely to become artists or it is possible that being an artist promotes these kinds of personality traits. For example, it is possible that the challenges of finding monetary success and recognition lead artists to become more aggressive and tough-minded.

Another way to study personality is to compare adults who engage in different careers, each of which can be creative in its own way. For example, a comparison of artists and creative scientists indicate that creative scientists are, in general, more autonomous, introverted, open to new experiences, self-confident, self-accepting, driven, ambitious, dominant, hostile, and impulsive. Artists tend to have more emotional instability and coldness in their personalities, and reject group norms more often than creative scientists.[14] To go one step further and compare musicians and visual artists (painters, sculptors, etc.), we find there are even differences between these groups-- particularly in extroversion and agreeableness. Musicians tend to be more extroverted and agreeable than visual artists.[15] This means that, in general, musicians like to be around other people and get along with other people to a greater extent than visual artists.

Although some of the personality characteristics seem to be rather negative, it would be a mistake to interpret them as such. One way to think about artists is that they are simply "more." They have strong personalities that are at more extreme ends of the normal range. As Frank Barron put it in 1963:

> *Thus the creative genius may be at once naïve and knowledgeable, being at home equally to primitive symbolism and to rigorous logic. He [sic] is both more primitive and more cultured, more destructive and more constructive,*

occasionally crazier and yet adamantly saner, than the average person.[16]

It is possible that there is such social discouragement of creative lives that only strong personalities can withstand the pressure into adulthood.[17] Although there is a general perception of the "crazy artist" this is not an accurate picture of this group of individuals. Most artists are in the normal range of possible personality factors.

Implications for the Classroom

From an educational standpoint the first thing to remember is to let go of stereotypes about the personalities of artistic individuals. Secondly, teachers might reflect on the fact that there are personality characteristics that are adaptive in the world of professional artistic creation that are not necessarily pleasant in the classroom. Introversion, emotional instability, and the rejection of group norms can create tension in the classroom. Resist the temptation to react judgmentally when encountering a student who seems "prickly" and is not necessary comfortable with the structure of schooling. Personality is changeable, so students can develop, but at the same time we wish for all students to feel comfortable in their own skins. Future artists are going to need to be strong and self-confident in order to weather the challenges that come as a result of being a professional in the arts.

AESTHETICS AND PERSONALITY

The pleasure of a creative life is second only to the pleasure that visual artists, musicians, and actors bring to the society at large. And it is not just pleasure, but the full range of emotions that are elicited by art, music, and performance. People like music, art, and film, although psychologists are far from a complete understanding of why humans like or dislike certain works despite the fact that the arts have been part of human existence for tens of thousands of years. The fact that experiencing music and the other arts is part of being human suggests that these endeavors must have some type of adaptive function. Psychologists are curious about how people use visual arts, theater and music in their lives and why they seek these experiences.

Music is the form of the arts that has been part of the human experience for the longest period of time. There is no single accepted theory that explains musical preference. But we do know some things that affect preference such as the musical characteristics of tempo, mode, and complexity as well as environmental factors such as the age, gender, personality, and education of the listener. The cognitive functions are important. People prefer music that conveys information about their identity and enhances bonding with others.[18] People tend to like music that matches their personality. For example, if a person has a perception of self as rebellious then music that expresses rebellion would be appealing. It would not only be in sync with perceived personality but it would also let others know that one is really rebellious at heart.

Most of the work on preferences for visual arts has also focused on personality dimensions. People who are generally open to new experience are also those who like visual art in general. But personality is not a particularly powerful predictor of what artworks a person will like. Even less work has been completed on preference for different theatrical works. Initial research suggests that preference for a theatrical work is a function of four dimensions (perceptive, cognitive, emotional, and communicative) with cognitive and emotional dimensions being the best predictors.[19] This means that we tend to enjoy works that stimulate our thinking about an idea and those that create an emotion in us that we seek to feel.

Examination of the effect of personality on aesthetic preferences often assumes that personality is a determining factor; meaning that one's personality determines one's preferences. This would be considered a top-down approach with personality on top and working down to preferences. But there is another perspective. It is possible that aesthetic choices such as music selection changes personality- a bottom-up approach. For example, a person who listens to a great many sad songs will become a sad person. Psychologists wonder how sounds, which are just acoustical waves, have the power to profoundly affect people. There are some universal findings. The major and minor modes of music as well as tempo are consistently connected to emotion with the fast and major mode seeming happy and slow and minor mode seeming sad. Humans seem to connect and label certain sounds with certain emotions. But people can label a song as being happy or sad without feeling that emotion. Aesthetics and emotion is interesting because several psychological theories of emotion involve the idea that different emotions were evolved to solve evolutionary problems.[20] But emotion connected with music, visual arts, and the theater is not connected to any real adaptive goal; they have no obvious survival value.

There is debate whether the emotions felt during aesthetic experiences are the same as emotions felt due to other experiences. Factors related to the emotional reaction to music range from the biological to the conceptual. Juslin & Västfäll[21] propose several possible dimensions. It is possible that there is a brain stem reflex related to discordant sounds. It is possible that people are conditioned to connect certain sounds with certain emotions as a result of experience. It is possible that emotion is induced because the listener perceives the emotional expression of the music and mimics this expression internally. It is possible that emotions related to music are the result of memories of past events connected to that music. It is likely that all these play a part in some way. There is also the possibility that we immerse ourselves in music, art and theater that evokes emotion in order to feel that emotion in a safe environment.[22] We wish to feel sadness without a negative experience that also causes anxiety. We wish to be scared without being in actual peril. There are many possibilities.

Implications for the Classroom

Even though few students will be able to make a living as an artist, remember that almost all people enjoy singing, art, and the theatre. Immerse all of your students in the possibilities of the arts. Explore, explore, explore. And then explore some more. Make sure that your students experience as many different forms of art and music as is possible. Use music to create a class bond. Create a classroom culture that involves art and music as part of the daily routine. For example, integrate a time in your schedule as you transition from one academic discipline to another (i.e., from Language Arts to Math perhaps) where the class listens to a 3-4 minute song and dances. This music will become "our class music" and will help create a classroom community. Use music to evoke emotion and link these to curricular goals.

For example, the CD *Here Comes Science* by the artists *They Might Be Giants* is a great way to link music and several key topics of science. Students can discuss both the content and how the music makes them feel thus creating stronger bonds in their minds and enhancing memory. Music can also be used to change the emotional climate in the classroom. If you want a calm classroom, play calm music. If you want to energize the students in the afternoon, then pump up the beat. Music can also be used as a signal for a particular time of the day. Play one genre of music, such as classical piano, when the students are taking tests or doing other silent and independent work, and choose another genre, such as jazz, when students are first entering the room. When the music is stopped or changed, students will know that it is time to transition to the next activity. Many students can recognize music from their favorite movies and television shows. In an English class, initiate a discussion about how the music affects the feelings of the viewers. For example, a video clip of one of the climactic scenes of an action movie, such as Jaws, will be understood quite differently if watched without the background music. Students might be asked to put together their own soundtracks for books they are reading and explain why the music they have chosen fits with certain parts of the book and how it would evoke the desired emotions in the listener.

Keep in mind that individuals like artistic works that stimulate feelings that one wants to feel. What do elementary children want to feel? Happiness. Humor. Excitement. For the elementary school teacher this means that one will be most successful with works that are funny, have happy endings, and involve a lot of movement. Most primary and elementary school teachers understand this intuitively. Adolescents are going to wish to experience more sadness and angst in their interaction with music, art, and theatre. This is reasonable. It allows adolescents to explore negative emotions in a safe way and among their peers. Connections are made when they understand that these feelings are shared by their peers. People like works that make them think about a topic that they want to think about. This also makes intuitive sense, but often as teachers we are disappointed that a play is not appreciated by our student audience. We need to step back and make sure that we have prepared the students so that they are primed to discuss the issue of the work before experiencing it.

The arts in all its forms inspire emotion. Consider an exploration in the classroom of the different emotions experienced by different students. Have students experience art or music or theatre and then discuss the emotions that they felt. What was similar? What was different? Why? This kind of explicit discussion of the experiences of art brings together the entire classroom whether they are producers of art or not. Harness the connection between emotion and music in order to accomplish instructional goals. Ask students questions such as, "What kind of song would remind you of Roman centurions?" and "If this book were a painting what would it look like?" For younger children you would probe with questions focused more on the actions associated with emotion and with older students you would focus more on the abstract emotions.

CONCLUSION

Psychology is at the foundation of human behavior including learning and development in the classroom. An understanding of the psychological principles and their applications allow teachers to base their practices in science. The arts are for everyone and extend throughout the instructional day, not just in special rooms or for special students. They are an integral part of the human experience that can be harnessed not only to enrich students but also to engage students in the day-to-day content and skills we wish students to learn. At the same time, teachers have a responsibility to facilitate the growth of potential artistic contributors. It is not easy to predict who these students will be, so when a little bud presents itself, we need to nurture it. From a psychological perspective this is accomplished by structuring experiences to provide for exploration, stressing the importance of practice and mastery of basic skills, and then giving the older student the courage to try. Respect the arts and the children who engage in them by embracing their potential in your classroom.

ENDNOTES

[1] Arnheim, R. (1954). *Art and visual perception: A psychology of the creative eye.* Berkeley: University of California Press.

[2] Kozbelt, A., Seidel, A., ElBassiouny, A., Mark, Y. & Owen, D. R. (2010). Visual selection contributes to artists' advantages in realistic drawing. *Psychology of Aesthetics, Creativity, and the Arts, 4,* 93-102.

[3] Noice, T., & Noice, H. (2002). The expertise of professional actors: A review of recent research. *High Ability Studies, 13,* 7-19; Noice, H., & Noice, T. (2006). What studies of actors and acting can tell us about memory and cognitive functioning. *Current Directions in Psychological Science, 15,* 14-18.

[4] Goldstein, T. R., & Winner, E. (2009). Living in alternative and inner worlds: Early signs of acting talent. *Creativity Research Journal, 21,* 117-124.

[5] Corrigall, K. A. & Trainor, L. J. (2010). Musical enculturation in preschool children: Acquisition of key and harmonic knowledge. *Music Perception: An Interdisciplinary Journal, 28,* 195-200.

[6] For more information about Readers Theater see http://www.scholastic.com/librarians/programs/whatisrt.htm

[7] For more information about the RAFT technique see http://www.readwritethink.org/professional-development/strategy-guides/using-raft-writing-strategy-30625.html#research-basis

[8] Sotiropoulou-Zormpala, M. (2012). Reflections on aesthetic teaching. *Art Education, 65,* 6-10.

[9] Sprague, M. M., & Bryan, S. L. (2001). Aesthetics and the middle school learner. *The Clearing House, 75,* 41-44.

[10] Princeton University Center for Arts and Cultural Policy Studies. (n.d.). *How many artists are there?* Retrieved from http://www.princeton.edu/~artspol/quickfacts/artists/artistemploy.html

[11] Ericsson, K. A., Charness, H., Feltovich, P. J., & Hoffman, R. R. (2006). *The Cambridge handbook of expertise and expert performance.* New York, NY: Cambridge University Press.

[12]Kogan, N. (2002). Careers in the performing arts: A psychological perspective. *Creativity Research Journal, 14*, 1-15.

[13]Batey, M., Chamorro-Premusic, T., & Furnham, A. (2010). Individual differences in ideational behavior: Can the big five and psychometric intelligence predict creativity scores? *Creativity and Research Journal, 22*, 90-97; Eysenck, H. J. (1993). Creativity and Personality: Suggestions for a theory. *Psychological Inquiry, 4*, 147-178; Feist, G. J. (1998). A meta-analysis of personality in scientific and artistic creativity. *Personality and Social Psychology Review, 2*, 290-309; Nettle, D. (2006). Psychological profiles of professional actors. *Personality and Individual Differences, 40*, 375-383.

[14]Feist, G. J., & Barron, F. X. (2003). Predicting creativity from early to late adulthood: Intellect, potential, and personality. *Journal of Research in Personality, 37*, 62-88.

[15]Haller, C. S., & Courvoisier, D. S. (2010). Personality and thinking style in different creative domains. Psychology of Aesthetics, *Creativity, and the Arts, 4*, 149-160.

[16]Barron, F. (1963). *Creativity and psychological health* (p. 224). Princeton, NJ: Van Nostrand.

[17]Eysenck, H. J. (1993). Creativity and personality: Suggestions for a theory. *Psychological Inquiry, 4*, 147-178.

[18]Schafer, T., & Sedmeir, P. (2010). What makes us like music? Determinants of music preference. *Psychology of Aesthetics, Creativity and the Arts, 4*, 223-234

[19]Boerner, S., Jobst, J., & Wiemann, M. (2010). Exploring the theatrical experience: Results from an empirical investigation. *Psychology of Aesthetics, Creativity, and the Arts, 4*, 173-180; Eversmann, P. (2004). The experience of the theatrical event. In V.A. Cremona, P. Eversmann, H. van Maanen, W. Sauter & J. Tulloch (Eds.), *Theatrical events. Borders –dynamics – frames* (pp. 139–174). Amsterdam, the Netherlands: Rodopi.

[20]LeDoux J. E. (2002). Emotion, memory, and the brain. *Scientific American, 12*, 62-71.

[21]Juslin, P. N., & Västfäll, D. (2008). Emotional responses to music: The need to consider underlying mechanisms. *Behavioral and Brain Sciences, 31*, 559-621.

[22]Goldstein, T. R. (2009). Psychological perspective on acting. *Psychology of Aesthetics, Creativity, and the Arts, 3*, 6-9.

KEY RESOURCES

The National Art Education Association website has numerous resources about art education that can be applied to both the art education classroom and the general classroom. The website provides resources that may pull you in and engage you in exploring. It is well worth the time, particularly the Lesson Planning section that includes resources from across the Internet. http://www.arteducators.org/

If you are interested in furthering your knowledge about applying the psychology of the arts to your teaching, consider becoming an affiliate member of the **American Psychological Association Division 10: The Society for the Psychology of Aesthetics, Creativity and the Arts.** A brief article about the benefits can be found here: https://www.apa.org/monitor/apr06/closer.aspx

Explore the website for the **Society for Psychology in the Performing Arts** (SPPA) which is an organization devoted to the application of psychological research to the performing arts. There are pages for teachers, researchers, and clinicians. http://www.artspsych.org/

How to Think Straight about Psychology (7th ed.) by Keith E Stanovich is a well-respected book written for anyone who wants a jargon-free presentation of key psychological theories and ideas. It is ideal for individuals who do not have an extensive background in psychology and want to be able to differentiate between valid ideas and pseudoscience.

The National Endowment for the Humanities has a site, **Picturing America,** which contains links to paintings, cultures, architecture, fine crafts and photography as catalysts to study American culture, politics and history. In addition, the Teacher Resource Book and PowerPoint provide images for classroom use.
http://picturingamerica.neh.gov/index.php?sec=home

ABOUT THE AUTHORS

Erin Morris Miller, Ph.D., is an Assistant Professor of Psychology at Bridgewater College where she teaches Memory/Cognition, Cognitive Neuroscience, Statistics, and Creativity/Problem-Solving. She has held various posts in the NAGC Conceptual Foundations Network over the last ten years. Her current interests include modeling the way people think about giftedness and intelligence.

Rachael Sloan is a pre-service teacher gaining licensure in elementary and English as a Second Language education. While studying at Bridgewater College, her research has included the various methods of identification of English language learners (ELLs) for gifted programs. Upon graduation, she hopes to become a full-time teacher of ELLs.

ABOUT THE SERIES EDITOR

Cheryll M. Adams, Ph.D., is the Director Emerita of the Center for Gifted Studies and Talent Development at Ball State University. She has served on the Board of Directors of NAGC and has been president of the Indiana Association for the Gifted and the Association for the Gifted, Council for Exceptional Children.

Made in the USA
San Bernardino, CA
22 August 2016